Legacy

Study this Book of Instruction continually. Meditate on it day and night so you will be sure to obey everything written in it. Only then will you prosper and succeed in all you do.9 This is my command—be strong and courageous! Do not be afraid or discouraged. For the Lord your God is with you wherever you go."

Joshua 1:8-9 (NLT)

Dedication

Legacy is dedicated to its reader, the Sons and Daughters that will carry on a family name and create a Legacy of their own. My hope for you is that you make it through this entire book, reading everything in it and becoming the best and wisest you that you can be. For the great parents who want to raise good kids with a Biblical foundation, I'm dedicating this book to you as well. Thank you and continue to strive forward.

Book ISBN 978-1-7339949-6-5

Cover and interior design by Priceless Digital Media.

Table of contents

Wisdom for Everyday Living

Legacy

Introduction

There are plenty of people who believe the Holy Bible was only written for people to get right with God, go to Heaven and stay out of Hell. It does have a lot to do with that, but that's not all the Bible focuses on. It focuses on the true nature of mankind and the importance of having wisdom.

What Legacy brings to its readers is a parallel view of a wise person and an unwise person. A person who needs wisdom and a person who has wisdom. Legacy will help its readers better understand "The Why," "The Way," and "The Results" of making good decisions verses making bad decisions.

Legacy comes from a book in the Bible called Proverbs. Proverbs concentrates on wisdom more than any other book in the Bible. Benjamin D. Author chose Proverbs because it takes place in a setting with a father and his family sitting around him talking about the important things in life. The benefits and advantages of a being a wise person, and the consequences and disadvantages of being a person of no wisdom. Wisdom has no gender, no skin color, nor any excuses. The only thing wisdom has is truth.

As we go read through these next 31 chapters, take note of what stands out and makes sense to you. The unique thing about this book is that every time you read it, you'll learn something new no matter how many times you read it or how old you get. Do me a favor and keep this book in a special place and don't lose it. Let this be a book that you keep for a lifetime.

— Thanks,
Benjamin

Legacy

1

The Purpose of Proverbs

Proverbs 1

The Purpose of Proverbs

These are the proverbs of Solomon, David's son, king of Israel.

Their purpose is to teach people wisdom and discipline, to help them understand the insights of the wise.

Their purpose is to teach people to live disciplined and successful lives, to help them do what is right, just, and fair.

These proverbs will give insight to the simple, knowledge and discernment to the young.

Let the wise listen to these proverbs and become even wiser.

Let those with understanding receive guidance by exploring the meaning in these proverbs and parables, the words of the wise and their riddles.

Fear of the LORD is the foundation of true knowledge, but fools despise wisdom and discipline.

My child, listen when your father corrects you.

Don't neglect your mother's instruction.

What you learn from them will crown you with grace and be a chain of honor around your neck.

My child, if sinners entice you, turn your back on them!

They may say, "Come and join us.

Let's hide and kill someone!

Just for fun, let's ambush the innocent!

Let's swallow them alive, like the grave; let's swallow them whole, like those who go down to the pit of death.

Think of the great things we'll get!

The Father here is telling his son to honor his parents. As young kids we understand that you're getting to the age where you want to start making your own decisions!!!

So called friends, buddies, or boys at school

Steal their stuff

We'll fill our houses with all the stuff we take.

Come, throw in your lot with us; we'll all share the loot."

My child, don't go along with them!

Stay far away from their paths. They rush to commit evil deeds.

They hurry to commit murder. If a bird sees a trap being set, it knows to stay away.

But these people set an ambush for themselves; they are trying to get themselves killed.

Such is the fate of all who are greedy for money; it robs them of life.

Wisdom shouts in the streets.

She cries out in the public square.She calls to the crowds along the main street, to those gathered in front of the city gate:

"How long, you simpletons, will you insist on being simpleminded?

How long will you mockers relish your mocking?

How long will you fools hate knowledge?

Come and listen to my counsel. I'll share my heart with you and make you wise.

"I called you so often, but you wouldn't come.

Make a deal with us and join our group

The Bible says

Wisdom is like a person standing on the side of the road waving their arms trying to get you attention so that you won't go the wrong way.

I reached out to you, but you paid no attention.

You ignored my advice and rejected the correction I offered.

So I will laugh when you are in trouble!

I will mock you when disaster overtakes you— when calamity overtakes you like a storm, when disaster engulfs you like a cyclone, and anguish and distress overwhelm you.

"When they cry for help, I will not answer.

Though they anxiously search for me, they will not find me.

For they hated knowledge and chose not to fear the LORD.

They rejected my advice and paid no attention when I corrected them.

Therefore, they must eat the bitter fruit of living their own way, choking on their own schemes.

For simpletons turn away from me—to death.

Fools are destroyed by their own complacency.

But all who listen to me will live in peace, untroubled by fear of harm."

This is a picture of how the world turns on you once you decide to follow it. Your parents or those in charge of you want to help you before all this happens to you because it will.

~NOTE SECTION~

Listen and Be Wise

Proverbs 2

The Benefits of Wisdom

My child, listen to what I say,
and treasure my commands.

Tune your ears to wisdom, and
concentrate on understanding.

Cry out for insight, and ask for
understanding.

Search for them as you would
for <u>silver</u>; seek them like <u>hidden
treasures</u>.

Or something you see as valuable

The right pair of shoes

Then you will understand what it means to fear the LORD, and you will gain knowledge of God.

For the LORD grants wisdom!

From his mouth come knowledge and understanding.

He grants a treasure of <u>common sense</u> to the honest.

He is a shield to those who walk with integrity.

He guards the paths of the just and protects those who are faithful to him.

Then you will understand what is right, just, and fair, and you will find the right way to go.

For wisdom will enter your heart, and knowledge will fill you with joy.

Wise choices will watch over you.

Understanding will keep you safe.

Wisdom will save you from <u>evil people, from those whose words are twisted.</u>

These men turn from the right way to walk down dark paths.

They take pleasure in doing wrong, and they enjoy the twisted ways of evil.

Their actions are crooked, and their ways are wrong.

Common sense is very important. It will help you tell right from wrong, good from bad.

Being good when no one is watching.

He watches out for you even when you don't think you need it.

Remember this

These are ways to tell the difference between good friend and bad friends.

They will always try to get you to do or think about doing drugs or look at porn and get you to drink or smoke or vape

The Bible says

Wisdom will save you from the immoral woman, from the seductive words of the promiscuous woman.

She has abandoned her husband and ignores the covenant she made before God.

Entering her house leads to death; it is the road to the grave.

The man who visits her is doomed.

He will never reach the paths of life.

So follow the steps of the good, and stay on the paths of the righteous.

For only the godly will live in the land, and those with integrity will remain in it.

But the wicked will be removed from the land, and the treacherous will be uprooted.

Fast and easy girls

The girl that says if you do this for me I will do that for you

Things to know about women when you get older

~NOTE SECTION~

3

Trusting in the Lord

Proverbs 3

My child, never forget the things I have taught you.

Store my commands in your heart.

If you do this, you will live many years, and your life will be satisfying.

Never let loyalty and kindness leave you!

Tie them around your neck as a reminder. Write them deep within your heart.

> Always be respectful to people or good as you can anyway.

> Put them in the Notes app in you phone or take a picture and look at it every now and then.

Then you will find favor with both God and people, and you will earn a good reputation.

Trust in the LORD with all your heart; do not depend on your own understanding.

Seek his will in all you do, and he will show you which path to take.

Don't be impressed with your own wisdom.

Instead, fear the LORD and turn away from evil.

Then you will have healing for your body and strength for your bones.

The right people will like you at the right time

Honor the LORD with your wealth and with the best part of everything you produce.

Then he will fill your barns with grain, and your vats will overflow with good wine.

Something to know when you are older

Your barn is your bank account your grain is your money Vats is a refrigerator.

My child, don't reject the LORD's discipline, and don't be upset when he corrects you.

For the LORD corrects those he loves, just as a father corrects a child in whom he delights.

Joyful is the person who finds wisdom, the one who gains understanding.

AS you get older, you will understand the Lord's discipline.

For wisdom is more profitable than silver, and her wages are better than gold.

In this section this is a parent and child discussion section. Dads talk and explain how you see these verses.

Wisdom is more precious than rubies; nothing you desire can compare with her.

She offers you long life in her right hand, and riches and honor in her left.

She will guide you down delightful paths; all her ways are satisfying.

Wisdom is a tree of life to those who embrace her; happy are those who hold her tightly.

By wisdom the LORD founded the earth; by understanding he created the heavens.

By his knowledge the deep fountains of the earth burst forth, and the dew settles beneath the night sky.

My child, don't lose sight of common sense and <u>discernment</u>.

Being able to look at a situation and know what to do without taking a long time to figure it out.

Hang on to them, for they will refresh your soul.

They are like jewels on a necklace.

They keep you safe on your way, and your feet will not stumble.

You can go to bed without fear; you will lie down and sleep soundly.

You need not be afraid of sudden disaster or the destruction that comes upon the wicked, for the LORD is your security.

He will keep your foot from being caught in a trap.

Do not withhold good from those who deserve it when it's in your power to help them.

If you can help your neighbor now, don't say, "Come back tomorrow, and then I'll help you."

Don't plot harm against your neighbor, for those who live nearby trust you.

Don't pick a fight without reason, when no one has done you harm.

Don't envy violent people or copy their ways.

Such wicked people are detestable to the LORD, but he offers his friendship to the godly.

The LORD curses the house of the wicked, but he blesses the home of the upright.

The LORD mocks the mockers but is gracious to the humble.

The wise inherit honor, but fools are put to shame!

Stop enjoying watching people fight on youtube.

~NOTE SECTION~

A Father's Advice

Proverbs 4

A Father's Wise Advice

My children, listen when your father corrects you.

Pay attention and learn good judgment, for I am giving you good guidance.

Don't turn away from my instructions.

For I, too, was once my father's son, tenderly loved as my mother's only child.

> We ourselves as parents was once our father's son, tenderly loved as my mother's child. So we can relate

My father taught me, "Take my words to heart.

Follow my commands, and you will live.

Get wisdom; develop good judgment.

Don't forget my words or turn away from them.

Don't turn your back on wisdom, for she will protect you.

Love her, and she will guard you.

Getting wisdom is the wisest thing you can do!

And whatever else you do, develop good judgment.

If you prize wisdom, she will make you great.

Embrace her, and she will honor you.

She will place a lovely wreath on your head; she will present you with a beautiful crown."

My child, listen to me and do as I say, and you will have a long, good life.

I will teach you wisdom's ways and lead you in straight paths.

When you walk, you won't be held back; when you run, you won't stumble.

I didn't always want to, but I listened anyway

You may not always feel like it, but it's for your own good to listen.

Value, respect, and want wisdom for yourself.

Crown for your head like a King.

Take hold of my instructions; don't let them go.

Guard them, for they are the key to life.

Don't do as the wicked do, and don't follow the path of evildoers.

Don't even think about it; don't go that way.

Turn away and keep moving.

For evil people can't sleep until they've done their evil deed for the day.

They can't rest until they've caused someone to stumble.

They eat the food of wickedness and drink the wine of violence!

The way of the righteous is like the first gleam of dawn, which shines ever brighter until the full light of day.

But the way of the wicked is like total darkness.

They have no idea what they are stumbling over.

My child, pay attention to what I say.

Listen carefully to my words.

Don't lose sight of them.

Let them penetrate deep into your heart, for they bring life to those who find them, and healing to their whole body.

Wisdom will open doors for you.

These are promised of God

Guard your heart above all else, for it determines the course of your life.

Avoid all perverse talk; stay away from corrupt speech.

Look straight ahead, and fix your eyes on what lies before you.

Mark out a straight path for your feet; stay on the safe path.

Don't get sidetracked; keep your feet from following evil.

Negative, strange, and inappropriate conversations

Prosperity, Goals, Good Grades, and a Good Life

~NOTE SECTION~

5

Fast Girls and a Future Wife

Proverbs 5

Avoid Immoral Women

My son, pay attention to my wisdom; listen carefully to my wise counsel.

Then you will show discernment, and your lips will express what you've learned.

For the lips of an immoral woman are as sweet as honey, and her mouth is smoother than oil.

> In this story a father is talking to his son, but girls should watch out for an immoral man just like a son should look out for an immoral girl or woman.

> She's a smooth talker, meaning she knows exactly what to say to men to get them to so exactly what she wants them to do.

But in the end she is as bitter as poison, as dangerous as a double-edged sword.

Her feet go down to death; her steps lead straight to the grave.

For she cares nothing about the path to life.

She staggers down a crooked trail and doesn't realize it.

So now, my sons, listen to me.

Never stray from what I am about to say:

Stay away from her!

Don't go near the door of her house!

If you do, you will lose your honor and will lose to merciless people all you have achieved.

Strangers will consume your wealth, and someone else will enjoy the fruit of your labor.

In the end you will groan in anguish when disease consumes your body.

You will say, "How I hated discipline!

If only I had not ignored all the warnings!

Oh, why didn't I listen to my teachers?

Why didn't I pay attention to my instructors?

> No matter how you handle her she can cut you

> This is a story from a man who has experienced a woman like this. He's kind of overexaggerating but, stilling the tell the truth at the same time so you can get the picture

> Merciless people has no pity on you or for you.

> All adults have said similar things

I have come to the brink of utter ruin, and now I must face public disgrace."

Drink water from your own well—share your love only with your wife.

Why spill the water of your springs in the streets, having sex with just anyone?

You should reserve it for yourselves.

Never share it with strangers.

Let your wife be a fountain of blessing for you.

Rejoice in the wife of your youth.

She is a loving deer, a graceful doe.

Let her breasts satisfy you always.

May you always be captivated by her love.

Why be captivated, my son, by an immoral woman, or fondle the breasts of a promiscuous woman?

For the LORD sees clearly what a man does, examining every path he takes.

Things to know or do when you are older

Say a virgin, don't see it as a good thing to have sex before marriage.

An evil man is held captive by his own sins; they are ropes that catch and hold him.

He will die for lack of self-control; he will be lost because of his great foolishness.

Porn, alcohol, gambling, drugs, and having sex with multiple women.

Ask your dad or whoever get you reading this book to give you examples of this kind of man and if he knows of one,

~NOTE SECTION~

Money Issues

Debt, Laziness, Hard Work, Wicked, and Lying People

Proverbs 6

Lessons for Daily Life

My child, if you have put up security for a friend's debt or agreed to guarantee the debt of a stranger—if you have trapped yourself by your agreement and are caught by what you said—follow my advice and save yourself, for you have placed yourself at your friend's mercy.

Now swallow your pride; go and beg to have your name erased.

Don't put it off; do it now!

Don't rest until you do.

Save yourself like a gazelle escaping from a hunter, like a bird fleeing from a net.

Take a lesson from the ants, you lazybones.

Learn from their ways and become wise!

Though they have no prince or governor or ruler to make them work, they labor hard all summer, gathering food for the winter.

But you, lazybones, how long will you sleep?

When will you wake up?

A little extra sleep, a little more slumber, a little folding of the hands to rest—then poverty will pounce on you like a bandit; scarcity will attack you like an armed robber.

Scarcity is the fear of running out of something you need or like.

. . . .

What are worthless and wicked people like?

They are constant liars, signaling their deceit with a wink of the eye, a nudge of the foot, or the wiggle of fingers.

Their perverted hearts plot evil,
and they constantly stir up trouble.
But they will be destroyed suddenly,
broken in an instant beyond all
hope of healing.

There are six things the LORD
hates—no, seven things he detests:

1. haughty eyes,
2. a lying tongue,
3. hands that kill the innocent,
4. a heart that plots evil,
5. feet that race to do wrong,
6. a false witness who pours out
   lies,
7. a person who sows discord in
   a family.

My son, obey your father's
commands, and don't neglect your
mother's instruction.

Keep their words always in your
heart.

Tie them around your neck.

When you walk, their counsel
will lead you.

When you sleep, they will
protect you.

When you wake up, they will
advise you.

For their command is a lamp and their instruction a light; their corrective discipline is the way to life.

It will keep you from the immoral woman, from the smooth tongue of a promiscuous woman.

Don't lust for her beauty.

Don't let her coy glances seduce you.

For a prostitute will bring you to poverty, but sleeping with another man's wife will cost you your life.

Can a man scoop a flame into his lap and not have his clothes catch on fire?

Can he walk on hot coals and not blister his feet?

So it is with the man who sleeps with another man's wife.

He who embraces her will not go unpunished.

A prostitute is a woman who sells herself in sexual activity for money.

This is a bad mistake people make.

Excuses might be found for a thief who steals because he is starving.

But if he is caught, he must pay back seven times what he stole, even if he has to sell everything in his house.

But the man who commits adultery is an utter fool, for he destroys himself.

He will be wounded and disgraced.

His shame will never be erased.

For the woman's jealous husband will be furious, and he will show no mercy when he takes revenge.

He will accept no compensation, nor be satisfied with a payoff of any size.

These are somethings every man should know, and if you're a young lady don't cheat on your husband.

~NOTE SECTION~

7

A Careless Man's Actions

Proverbs 7

Another Warning about Immoral Women

Follow my advice, my son; always treasure my commands. Obey my commands and live!

Guard my instructions as you guard your own eyes.

Tie them on your fingers as a reminder.

Write them deep within your heart.

Love wisdom like a sister; make insight a beloved member of your family.

Let them protect you from an <u>affair</u> with an immoral woman, from listening to the flattery of a promiscuous woman.

Being involved

Smooth talking fast - acting woman

A promiscuous woman is a woman who has sex a lot and with different men.

· · · · · · · · ·

While I was at the window of my house, looking through the curtain, I saw some <u>naive</u> young men, and one in particular who lacked common sense.

Simple minded and trusting anything he hears man.

He was crossing the street near the house of an immoral woman, strolling down the path by her house.

It was at twilight, in the evening, as deep darkness fell.

It was about dark

The woman approached him, seductively dressed and sly of heart.

She was the brash, rebellious type, never content to stay at home.

She is often in the streets and markets, soliciting at every corner.

She threw her arms around him and kissed him, and with a brazen look she said,

"I've just made my peace offerings and fulfilled my vows.

She paid her bills and now she doesn't have a care in the world.

You're the one I was looking for!

I came out to find you, and here you are!

My bed is spread with beautiful blankets, with colored sheets of Egyptian linen.

I've perfumed my bed with myrrh, aloes, and cinnamon.

Come, let's drink our fill of love until morning.

Let's enjoy each other's <u>caresses</u>, for my husband is not home.

He's away on a long trip.

He has taken a wallet full of money with him and won't return until later this month."

So she seduced him with her pretty speech and enticed him with her flattery.

He followed her at once, like an ox going to the slaughter.

He was like a stag caught in a trap, awaiting the arrow that would pierce its heart.

He was like a bird flying into a snare, little knowing it would cost him his life.

So listen to me, my sons, and pay attention to my words.

Now she says

She never met this guy before but she's telling him, she's been waiting for him.

Have sex until morning.

Bodies

Red Flag #1: She's married.

Red Flag #2: they still live together.

Red Flag #3: he's coming back, but she doesn't exactly know when.

Most men will fall for this type of woman if he gets too close to her.

When an ox or cow is lead to the slaughter, they walk straight with their head down not seeing where they are going.

A stag is s male deer

A snare is a net used to catch animals.

Don't let your hearts stray away toward her.

Don't wander down her wayward path.

For she has been the ruin of many; many men have been her victims.

Her house is the road to the grave.

Her bedroom is the den of death.

Many good men.

~NOTE SECTION~

8

When Wisdom Calls Out

Proverbs 8

Wisdom Calls for a Hearing

1 Listen as Wisdom calls out! Hear
as understanding raises her voice!

2 On the hilltop along the road, she
takes her stand at the crossroads.

3 By the gates at the entrance to the
town, on the road leading in, she
cries aloud,

4 "I call to you, to all of you! I raise
my voice to all people.

5 You simple people, use good judgment. You foolish people, show some understanding.

6 Listen to me! For I have important things to tell you. Everything I say is right,

7 for I speak the truth and detest every kind of deception.

To detest something is to not like it

8 My advice is wholesome. There is nothing devious or crooked in it.

Wholesome is something being good for you.

9 My words are plain to anyone with understanding, clear to those with knowledge.

10 Choose my instruction rather than silver, and knowledge rather than pure gold.

11 For wisdom is far more valuable than rubies. Nothing you desire can compare with it.

12 "I, Wisdom, live together with good judgment. I know where to discover knowledge and discernment.

This won't happen overnight, but rather a life-time to accomplish. So stay Humble

13 All who fear the LORD will hate evil. Therefore, I hate pride and arrogance, corruption and perverse speech.

Cursing and really bad trash talking.

14 Common sense and success belong to me. Insight and strength are mine.

15 Because of me, kings reign, and
rulers make just decrees.

16 Rulers lead with my help,
and nobles make righteous
judgments.

17 "I love all who love me. Those
who search will surely find me.

18 I have riches and honor, as well
as enduring wealth and justice.

19 My gifts are better than gold,
even the purest gold, my wages
better than sterling silver!

20 I walk in righteousness, in paths
of justice.

21 Those who love me inherit
wealth. I will fill their treasuries.

22 "The LORD formed me from
the beginning, before he created
anything else.

23 I was appointed in ages past, at
the very first, before the earth
began.

24 I was born before the oceans
were created, before the springs
bubbled forth their waters.

25 Before the mountains were formed,
before the hills, I was born—

26 before he had made the earth
and fields and the first handfuls
of soil.

27 I was there when he established
the heavens, when he drew the
horizon on the oceans.

Really good advice

28 I was there when he set the clouds above, when he established springs deep in the earth.

29 I was there when he set the limits of the seas, so they would not spread beyond their boundaries. And when he marked off the earth's foundations,

30 I was the architect at his side. I was his constant delight, rejoicing always in his presence.

31 And how happy I was with the world he created; how I rejoiced with the human family!

32 "And so, my children, listen to me, for all who follow my ways are joyful.

33 Listen to my instruction and be wise. Don't ignore it.

34 Joyful are those who listen to me, watching for me daily at my gates, waiting for me outside my home!

35 For whoever finds me finds life and receives favor from the LORD.

36 But those who miss me injure themselves. All who hate me love death."

~NOTE SECTION~

Legacy

Wise Actions

Proverbs 9

1 Wisdom has built her house; she has carved its seven columns.
2 She has prepared a great banquet, mixed the wines, and set the table.
3 She has sent her servants to invite everyone to come. She calls out from the heights overlooking the city.

4 "Come in with me," she urges the simple. To those who lack good judgment, she says,

5 "Come, eat my food, and drink the wine I have mixed.

6 Leave your simple ways behind, and begin to live; learn to use good judgment."

7 Anyone who rebukes a mocker will get an insult in return. Anyone who corrects the wicked will get hurt.

8 So don't bother correcting mockers; they will only hate you. But correct the wise, and they will love you.

9 Instruct the wise, and they will be even wiser. Teach the righteous, and they will learn even more.

10 Fear of the LORD is the foundation of wisdom. Knowledge of the Holy One results in good judgment.

11 Wisdom will multiply your days and add years to your life.

12 If you become wise, you will be the one to benefit. If you scorn wisdom, you will be the one to suffer.

This is my favorite verse.

Folly "Calls Out" for a Hearing

13 The woman named Folly is brash. She is ignorant and doesn't know it.

14 She sits in her doorway on the heights overlooking the city.

15 She calls out to men going by who are minding their own business.

16 "Come in with me," she urges the simple. To those who lack good judgment, she says,

17 "Stolen water is refreshing; food eaten in secret tastes the best!"

18 But little do they know that the dead are there. Her guests are in the depths of the grave.

~NOTE SECTION~

Money

Being Lazy vs Being Instructed

Proverbs 10

The Proverbs of Solomon

1 The proverbs of Solomon:
A wise child brings joy to a
father; a foolish child brings grief
to a mother.

2 Tainted wealth has no lasting
value, but right living can save
your life.

3 The LORD will not let the godly go hungry, but he refuses to satisfy the craving of the wicked.

4 Lazy people are soon poor; hard workers get rich.

5 A wise youth harvests in the summer, but one who sleeps during harvest is a disgrace.

6 The godly are showered with blessings; the words of the wicked conceal violent intentions.

7 We have happy memories of the godly, but the name of a wicked person rots away.

8 The wise are glad to be instructed, but babbling fools fall flat on their faces.

9 People with integrity walk safely, but those who follow crooked paths will be exposed.

10 People who wink at wrong cause trouble, but a bold reproof promotes peace.

11 The words of the godly are a life-giving fountain; the words of the wicked conceal violent intentions.

12 Hatred stirs up quarrels, but love makes up for all offenses.

13 Wise words come from the lips of people with understanding, but those lacking sense will be beaten with a rod.

A good verse to add to memory.

This is why it is important to be careful in whom you listen too.

14 Wise people treasure knowledge, but the babbling of a fool invites disaster.

15 The wealth of the rich is their fortress; ■ the poverty of the poor is their destruction.

16 The earnings of the godly enhance their lives, but evil people squander their money on sin.

17 People who accept discipline are on the pathway to life, but those who ignore correction will go astray.

18 Hiding hatred makes you a liar; slandering others makes you a fool.

19 Too much talk leads to sin. Be sensible and keep your mouth shut.

20 The words of the godly are like sterling silver; the heart of a fool is worthless.

21 The words of the godly encourage many, but fools are destroyed by their lack of common sense.

22 The blessing of the LORD makes a person rich, and he adds no sorrow with it.

23 Doing wrong is fun for a fool, but living wisely brings pleasure to the sensible.

Reading this book is a sign that you are:
· Reading the right thing.
· Going in the right direction.
· Learning the right information.

Remembering verses like these will help you in the future.

24 The fears of the wicked will be fulfilled; the hopes of the godly will be granted.

25 When the storms of life come, the wicked are whirled away, but the godly have a lasting foundation.

26 Lazy people irritate their employers, like vinegar to the teeth or smoke in the eyes.

27 Fear of the LORD lengthens one's life, but the years of the wicked are cut short.

28 The hopes of the godly result in happiness, but the expectations of the wicked come to nothing.

29 The way of the LORD is a stronghold to those with integrity, but it destroys the wicked.

30 The godly will never be disturbed, but the wicked will be removed from the land.

31 The mouth of the godly person gives wise advice, but the tongue that deceives will be cut off.

32 The lips of the godly speak helpful words, but the mouth of the wicked speaks perverse words.

You will notice that a lot of these verses will be for you in the future.

~NOTE SECTION~

Legacy

Honest People and an Honest Living

Proverbs 11

1 The LORD detests the use of dishonest scales, but he delights in accurate weights.

2 Pride leads to disgrace, but with humility comes wisdom.

3 Honesty guides good people; dishonesty destroys treacherous people.

4 Riches won't help on the day of judgment, but right living can save you from death.

5 The godly are directed by honesty; the wicked fall beneath their load of sin.

6 The godliness of good people rescues them; the ambition of treacherous people traps them.

7 When the wicked die, their hopes die with them, for they rely on their own feeble strength.

8 The godly are rescued from trouble, and it falls on the wicked instead.

9 With their words, the godless destroy their friends, but knowledge will rescue the righteous.

10 The whole city celebrates when the godly succeed; they shout for joy when the wicked die.

11 Upright citizens are good for a city and make it prosper, but the talk of the wicked tears it apart.

12 It is foolish to belittle one's neighbor; a sensible person keeps quiet.

13 A gossip goes around telling secrets, but those who are trustworthy can keep a confidence.

14 Without wise leadership, a nation falls; there is safety in having many advisers.

15 There's danger in putting up security for a stranger's debt; it's safer not to guarantee another person's debt.

16 A gracious woman gains respect, but ruthless men gain only wealth.

17 Your kindness will reward you, but your cruelty will destroy you.

18 Evil people get rich for the moment, but the reward of the godly will last.

19 Godly people find life; evil people find death.

20 The LORD detests people with crooked hearts, but he delights in those with integrity.

21 Evil people will surely be punished, but the children of the godly will go free.

22 A beautiful woman who lacks discretion is like a gold ring in a pig's snout.

23 The godly can look forward to a reward, while the wicked can expect only judgment.

24 Give freely and become more wealthy; be stingy and lose everything.

This is why we need a good President with good leadership.

25 The generous will prosper; those who refresh others will themselves be refreshed.

26 People curse those who hoard their grain, but they bless the one who sells in time of need.

27 If you search for good, you will find favor; but if you search for evil, it will find you!

28 Trust in your money and down you go! But the godly flourish like leaves in spring.

29 Those who bring trouble on their families inherit the wind. The fool will be a servant to the wise.

30 The seeds of good deeds become a tree of life; a wise person wins friends.

31 If the righteous are rewarded here on earth, what will happen to wicked sinners?

~NOTE SECTION~

Godly Outcomes and Wicked Outcomes

Proverbs 12

1 To learn, you must love discipline;
it is stupid to hate correction.

2 The LORD approves of those
who are good, but he condemns
those who plan wickedness.

3 Wickedness never brings stability,
but the godly have deep roots.

4 A worthy wife is a crown for
her husband, but a disgraceful
woman is like cancer in his

bones.

5 The plans of the godly are just;
the advice of the wicked is
treacherous.

6 The words of the wicked are like
a murderous ambush, but the
words of the godly save lives.

7 The wicked die and disappear, but
the family of the godly stands
firm.

8 A sensible person wins admiration,
but a warped mind is despised.

9 Better to be an ordinary person
with a servant than to be self-
important but have no food.

10 The godly care for their animals,
but the wicked are always cruel.

11 A hard worker has plenty of food,
but a person who chases fantasies
has no sense.

12 Thieves are jealous of each
other's loot, but the godly are well
rooted and bear their own fruit.

13 The wicked are trapped by their
own words, but the godly escape
such trouble.

14 Wise words bring many benefits,
and hard work brings rewards.

15 Fools think their own way is
right, but the wise listen to
others.

16 A fool is quick-tempered, but

a wise person stays calm when insulted.

17 An honest witness tells the truth; a false witness tells lies.

18 Some people make cutting remarks, but the words of the wise bring healing.

19 Truthful words stand the test of time, but lies are soon exposed.

20 Deceit fills hearts that are plotting evil; joy fills hearts that are planning peace!

21 No harm comes to the godly, but the wicked have their fill of trouble.

22 The LORD detests lying lips, but he delights in those who tell the truth.

23 The wise don't make a show of their knowledge, but fools broadcast their foolishness.

24 Work hard and become a leader; be lazy and become a slave.

25 Worry weighs a person down; an encouraging word cheers a person up.

26 The godly give good advice to their friends; the wicked lead them astray.

27 Lazy people don't even cook the game they catch, but the diligent make use of everything they find.

28 The way of the godly leads to life; that path does not lead to death.

Pick out 5 Outcomes and discuss them.
·
·
·
·
·

~NOTE SECTION~

13

Choices of the Wise and the Mistakes of the Unwise

Proverbs 13

1 A wise child accepts a parent's discipline; a mocker refuses to listen to correction.

2 Wise words will win you a good meal, but treacherous people have an appetite for violence.

3 Those who control their tongue will have a long life; opening your mouth can ruin everything.

4 Lazy people want much but get little, but those who work hard will prosper.

5 The godly hate lies; the wicked cause shame and disgrace.

6 Godliness guards the path of the blameless, but the evil are misled by sin.

7 Some who are poor pretend to be rich; others who are rich pretend to be poor.

8 The rich can pay a ransom for their lives, but the poor won't even get threatened.

9 The life of the godly is full of light and joy, but the light of the wicked will be snuffed out.

10 Pride leads to conflict; those who take advice are wise.

11 Wealth from get-rich-quick schemes quickly disappears; wealth from hard work grows over time.

12 Hope deferred makes the heart sick, but a dream fulfilled is a tree of life.

13 People who despise advice are asking for trouble; those who respect a command will succeed.

14 The instruction of the wise is like a life-giving fountain; those who accept it avoid the snares of death.

15 A person with good sense is respected; a treacherous person is headed for destruction.

16 Wise people think before they act; fools don't—and even brag about their foolishness.

17 An unreliable messenger stumbles into trouble, but a reliable messenger brings healing.

18 If you ignore criticism, you will end in poverty and disgrace; if you accept correction, you will be honored.

19 It is pleasant to see dreams come true, but fools refuse to turn from evil to attain them.

20 Walk with the wise and become wise; associate with fools and get in trouble.

21 Trouble chases sinners, while blessings reward the righteous.

22 Good people leave an inheritance to their grandchildren, but the sinner's wealth passes to the godly.

23 A poor person's farm may produce much food, but injustice sweeps it all away.

24 Those who spare the rod of discipline hate their children. Those who love their children care enough to discipline them.

25 The godly eat to their hearts' content, but the belly of the wicked goes hungry.

~NOTE SECTION~

Techniques of the Wise

Proverbs 14

1 A wise woman builds her home,
   but a foolish woman tears it
   down with her own hands.
2 Those who follow the right path
   fear the LORD; those who take
   the wrong path despise him.
3 A fool's proud talk becomes a rod
   that beats him, but the words of
   the wise keep them safe.

4 Without oxen a stable stays clean, but you need a strong ox for a large harvest.

5 An honest witness does not lie; a false witness breathes lies.

6 A mocker seeks wisdom and never finds it, but knowledge comes easily to those with understanding.

7 Stay away from fools, for you won't find knowledge on their lips.

8 The prudent understand where they are going, but fools deceive themselves.

9 Fools make fun of guilt, but the godly acknowledge it and seek reconciliation.

10 Each heart knows its own bitterness, and no one else can fully share its joy.

11 The house of the wicked will be destroyed, but the tent of the godly will flourish.

12 There is a path before each person that seems right, but it ends in death.

13 Laughter can conceal a heavy heart, but when the laughter ends, the grief remains.

14 Backsliders get what they deserve; good people receive their reward.

15 Only simpletons believe everything they're told! The prudent carefully consider their steps.

16 The wise are cautious and avoid danger; fools plunge ahead with reckless confidence.

17 Short-tempered people do foolish things, and schemers are hated.

18 Simpletons are clothed with foolishness, but the prudent are crowned with knowledge.

19 Evil people will bow before good people; the wicked will bow at the gates of the godly.

20 The poor are despised even by their neighbors, while the rich have many "friends."

21 It is a sin to belittle one's neighbor; blessed are those who help the poor.

22 If you plan to do evil, you will be lost; if you plan to do good, you will receive unfailing love and faithfulness.

23 Work brings profit, but mere talk leads to poverty!

24 Wealth is a crown for the wise; the effort of fools yields only foolishness.

25 A truthful witness saves lives, but a false witness is a traitor.

26 Those who fear the LORD are secure; he will be a refuge for their children

27 Fear of the LORD is a life-giving fountain; it offers escape from the snares of death.

28 A growing population is a king's glory; a prince without subjects has nothing.

29 People with understanding control their anger; a hot temper shows great foolishness.

30 A peaceful heart leads to a healthy body; jealousy is like cancer in the bones.

31 Those who oppress the poor insult their Maker, but helping the poor honors him.

32 The wicked are crushed by disaster, but the godly have a refuge when they die.

33 Wisdom is enshrined in an understanding heart; wisdom is not found among fools.

34 Godliness makes a nation great, but sin is a disgrace to any people.

35 A king rejoices in wise servants but is angry with those who disgrace him.

~NOTE SECTION~

Legacy

15

Reasons and Ways to Stay Calm, Cool, and Collective

Proverbs 15

1 A gentle answer deflects anger, but harsh words make tempers flare.

2 The tongue of the wise makes knowledge appealing, but the mouth of a fool belches out foolishness.

3 The LORD is watching everywhere, keeping his eye on both the evil and the good.

4 4 Gentle words are a tree of life; a deceitful tongue crushes the spirit.

5 5 Only a fool despises a parent's discipline; whoever learns from correction is wise.

6 6 There is treasure in the house of the godly, but the earnings of the wicked bring trouble.

7 7 The lips of the wise give good advice; the heart of a fool has none to give.

8 8 The LORD detests the sacrifice of the wicked, but he delights in the prayers of the upright.

9 9 The LORD detests the way of the wicked, but he loves those who pursue godliness.

10 Whoever abandons the right path will be severely disciplined; whoever hates correction will die.

11 Even Death and Destruction hold no secrets from the LORD. How much more does he know the human heart!

12 Mockers hate to be corrected, so they stay away from the wise.

13 A glad heart makes a happy face; a broken heart crushes the spirit.

14 A wise person is hungry for knowledge, while the fool feeds on trash.

15 For the despondent, every day brings trouble; for the happy heart, life is a continual feast.

16 Better to have little, with fear for the LORD, than to have great treasure and inner turmoil.

17 A bowl of vegetables with someone you love is better than steak with someone you hate.

18 A hot-tempered person starts fights; a cool-tempered person stops them.

19 A lazy person's way is blocked with briers, but the path of the upright is an open highway.

20 Sensible children bring joy to their father; foolish children despise their mother.

21 Foolishness brings joy to those with no sense; a sensible person stays on the right path.

22 Plans go wrong for lack of advice; many advisers bring success.

23 Everyone enjoys a fitting reply; it is wonderful to say the right thing at the right time!

24 The path of life leads upward for the wise; they leave the grave behind.

25 The LORD tears down the house of the proud, but he protects the property of widows.

26 The LORD detests evil plans, but he delights in pure words.

27 Greed brings grief to the whole family, but those who hate bribes will live.

28 The heart of the godly thinks carefully before speaking; the mouth of the wicked overflows with evil words.

29 The LORD is far from the wicked, but he hears the prayers of the righteous.

30 A cheerful look brings joy to the heart; good news makes for good health.

31 If you listen to constructive criticism, you will be at home among the wise.

32 If you reject discipline, you only harm yourself; but if you listen to correction, you grow in understanding.

33 Fear of the LORD teaches wisdom; humility precedes honor.

~NOTE SECTION~

16

Understanding Authority, Purpose, Plans, and Where You Stand

Proverbs 16

1 We can make our own plans,
but the LORD gives the right
answer.
2 People may be pure in their own
eyes, but the LORD examines
their motives.

This is a good
Buddy Chapter.

3 Commit your actions to the
   LORD, and your plans will
   succeed.

4 The LORD has made everything
   for his own purposes, even the
   wicked for a day of disaster.

5 The LORD detests the proud;
   they will surely be punished.

6 Unfailing love and faithfulness
   make atonement for sin. By
   fearing the LORD, people avoid
   evil.

7 When people's lives please the
   LORD, even their enemies are at
   peace with them.

8 Better to have little, with
   godliness, than to be rich and
   dishonest.

9 We can make our plans, but the
   LORD determines our steps.

10 The king speaks with divine
   wisdom; he must never judge
   unfairly.

11 The LORD demands accurate
   scales and balances; he sets the
   standards for fairness.

12 A king detests wrongdoing, for
   his rule is built on justice.

13 The king is pleased with words
   from righteous lips; he loves
   those who speak honestly.

14 The anger of the king is a deadly threat; the wise will try to appease it.

15 When the king smiles, there is life; his favor refreshes like a spring rain.

16 How much better to get wisdom than gold, and good judgment than silver!

17 The path of the virtuous leads away from evil; whoever follows that path is safe.

18 Pride goes before destruction, and haughtiness before a fall.

19 Better to live humbly with the poor than to share plunder with the proud.

20 Those who listen to instruction will prosper; those who trust the LORD will be joyful.

21 The wise are known for their understanding, and pleasant words are persuasive.

22 Discretion is a life-giving fountain to those who possess it, but discipline is wasted on fools.

23 From a wise mind comes wise speech; the words of the wise are persuasive.

24 Kind words are like honey— sweet to the soul and healthy for the body.

25 There is a path before each person that seems right, but it ends in death.

26 It is good for workers to have an appetite; an empty stomach drives them on.

27 Scoundrels create trouble; their words are a destructive blaze.

28 A troublemaker plants seeds of strife; gossip separates the best of friends.

29 Violent people mislead their companions, leading them down a harmful path.

30 With narrowed eyes, people plot evil; with a smirk, they plan their mischief.

31 Gray hair is a crown of glory; it is gained by living a godly life.

32 Better to be patient than powerful; better to have self-control than to conquer a city.

33 We may throw the dice, but the LORD determines how they fall.

~NOTE SECTION~

One Over the Other

Proverbs 17

1 Better a dry crust eaten in peace than a house filled with feasting—and conflict.

2 A wise servant will rule over the master's disgraceful son and will share the inheritance of the master's children.

3 Fire tests the purity of silver and gold, but the LORD tests the heart.

4 Wrongdoers eagerly listen to gossip; liars pay close attention to slander.

5 Those who mock the poor insult their Maker; those who rejoice at the misfortune of others will be punished.

6 Grandchildren are the crowning glory of the aged; parents are the pride of their children.

7 Eloquent words are not fitting for a fool; even less are lies fitting for a ruler.

8 A bribe is like a lucky charm; whoever gives one will prosper!

9 Love prospers when a fault is forgiven, but dwelling on it separates close friends.

10 A single rebuke does more for a person of understanding than a hundred lashes on the back of a fool.

11 Evil people are eager for rebellion, but they will be severely punished.

12 It is safer to meet a bear robbed of her cubs than to confront a fool caught in foolishness.

13 If you repay good with evil, evil will never leave your house.

We have to forgive people with love.

14 Starting a quarrel is like opening a floodgate, so stop before a dispute breaks out.

15 Acquitting the guilty and condemning the innocent— both are detestable to the LORD.

16 It is senseless to pay to educate a fool, since he has no heart for learning.

17 A friend is always loyal, and a brother is born to help in time of need.

18 It's poor judgment to guarantee another person's debt or put up security for a friend.

19 Anyone who loves to quarrel loves sin; anyone who trusts in high walls invites disaster.

20 The crooked heart will not prosper; the lying tongue tumbles into trouble.

21 It is painful to be the parent of a fool; there is no joy for the father of a rebel.

22 A cheerful heart is good medicine, but a broken spirit saps a person's strength.

23 The wicked take secret bribes to pervert the course of justice.

It is poor judgment to Co-Sign with someone.

24 Sensible people keep their eyes glued on wisdom, but a fool's eyes wander to the ends of the earth.

25 Foolish children bring grief to their father and bitterness to the one who gave them birth.

26 It is wrong to punish the godly for being good or to flog leaders for being honest.

27 A truly wise person uses few words; a person with understanding is even-tempered.

28 Even fools are thought wise when they keep silent; with their mouths shut, they seem intelligent.

~NOTE SECTION~

Legacy

Cause and Effect

Proverbs 18

1 Unfriendly people care only about themselves; they lash out at common sense.
2 Fools have no interest in understanding; they only want to air their own opinions.
3 Doing wrong leads to disgrace, and scandalous behavior brings contempt.

4 Wise words are like deep waters; wisdom flows from the wise like a bubbling brook.

5 It is not right to acquit the guilty or deny justice to the innocent.

6 Fools' words get them into constant quarrels; they are asking for a beating.

7 The mouths of fools are their ruin; they trap themselves with their lips.

8 Rumors are dainty morsels that sink deep into one's heart.

9 A lazy person is as bad as someone who destroys things.

10 The name of the LORD is a strong fortress; the godly run to him and are safe.

11 The rich think of their wealth as a strong defense; they imagine it to be a high wall of safety.

12 Haughtiness goes before destruction; humility precedes honor.

13 Spouting off before listening to the facts is both shameful and foolish.

14 The human spirit can endure a sick body, but who can bear a crushed spirit?

Haughtiness is also known as pride.

15 Intelligent people are always ready to learn. Their ears are open for knowledge.

16 Giving a gift can open doors; it gives access to important people!

17 The first to speak in court sounds right—until the cross-examination begins.

18 Flipping a coin can end arguments; it settles disputes between powerful opponents.

19 An offended friend is harder to win back than a fortified city. Arguments separate friends like a gate locked with bars.

20 Wise words satisfy like a good meal; the right words bring satisfaction.

21 The tongue can bring death or life; those who love to talk will reap the consequences.

22 The man who finds a wife finds a treasure, and he receives favor from the LORD.

23 The poor plead for mercy; the rich answer with insults.

24 There are "friends" who destroy each other, but a real friend sticks closer than a brother.

Note-to-self

~NOTE SECTION~

19

The Ways of Life

Proverbs 19

1 Better to be poor and honest than
   to be dishonest and a fool.
2 Enthusiasm without knowledge is
   no good; haste makes mistakes.
3 People ruin their lives by their
   own foolishness and then are
   angry at the LORD.
4 Wealth makes many "friends";
   poverty drives them all away.
5 A false witness will not go
   unpunished, nor will a liar escape.

*The way people of
the world thinks.*

6 Many seek favors from a ruler; everyone is the friend of a person who gives gifts!

7 The relatives of the poor despise them; how much more will their friends avoid them! Though the poor plead with them, their friends are gone.

8 To acquire wisdom is to love yourself; people who cherish understanding will prosper.

9 A false witness will not go unpunished, and a liar will be destroyed.

10 It isn't right for a fool to live in luxury or for a slave to rule over princes!

11 Sensible people control their temper; they earn respect by overlooking wrongs.

12 The king's anger is like a lion's roar, but his favor is like dew on the grass.

13 A foolish child is a calamity to a father; a quarrelsome wife is as annoying as constant dripping.

14 Fathers can give their sons an inheritance of houses and wealth, but only the LORD can give an understanding wife.

15 Lazy people sleep soundly, but idleness leaves them hungry.

16 Keep the commandments and keep your life; despising them leads to death.

17 If you help the poor, you are lending to the LORD— and he will repay you!

18 Discipline your children while there is hope. Otherwise you will ruin their lives.

19 Hot-tempered people must pay the penalty. If you rescue them once, you will have to do it again.

20 Get all the advice and instruction you can, so you will be wise the rest of your life.

21 You can make many plans, but the LORD's purpose will prevail.

22 Loyalty makes a person attractive. It is better to be poor than dishonest.

23 Fear of the LORD leads to life, bringing security and protection from harm.

24 Lazy people take food in their hand but don't even lift it to their mouth.

25 If you punish a mocker, the simpleminded will learn a lesson; if you correct the wise, they will be all the wiser.

26 Children who mistreat their
father or chase away their mother
are an embarrassment and a
public disgrace.

27 If you stop listening to
instruction, my child, you will
turn your back on knowledge.

28 A corrupt witness makes a
mockery of justice; the mouth of
the wicked gulps down evil.

29 Punishment is made for mockers,
and the backs of fools are made
to be beaten.

~NOTE SECTION~

Self-Defense for the Wise

Proverbs 20

1 Wine produces mockers; alcohol leads to brawls. Those led astray by drink cannot be wise.

2 The king's fury is like a lion's roar; to rouse his anger is to risk your life.

3 Avoiding a fight is a mark of honor; only fools insist on quarreling.

4 Those too lazy to plow in the right season will have no food at the harvest.

5 Though good advice lies deep within the heart, a person with understanding will draw it out.

6 Many will say they are loyal friends, but who can find one who is truly reliable?

7 The godly walk with integrity; blessed are their children who follow them.

8 When a king sits in judgment, he weighs all the evidence, distinguishing the bad from the good.

9 Who can say, "I have cleansed my heart; I am pure and free from sin"?

10 False weights and unequal measures—the LORD detests double standards of every kind.

11 Even children are known by the way they act, whether their conduct is pure, and whether it is right.

12 Ears to hear and eyes to see— both are gifts from the LORD.

13 If you love sleep, you will end in poverty. Keep your eyes open, and there will be plenty to eat!

Nobody

Don't be racist or anything like that.

Note-to-Self

Pray for these things

14 The buyer haggles over the price, saying, "It's worthless," then brags about getting a bargain!

Learn how to negotiate

15 Wise words are more valuable than much gold and many rubies.

16 Get security from someone who guarantees a stranger's debt. Get a deposit if he does it for foreigners.

17 Stolen bread tastes sweet, but it turns to gravel in the mouth.

Certain thrills aren't always worth the risk

18 Plans succeed through good counsel; don't go to war without wise advice.

You need a team, but your team must be a righteous team.

19 A gossip goes around telling secrets, so don't hang around with chatterers.

20 If you insult your father or mother, your light will be snuffed out in total darkness.

21 An inheritance obtained too early in life is not a blessing in the end.

Because you can waste it by being to immature.

22 Don't say, "I will get even for this wrong." Wait for the LORD to handle the matter.

23 The LORD detests double standards; he is not pleased by dishonest scales.

24 The LORD directs our steps, so why try to understand everything along the way?

25 Don't trap yourself by making
a rash promise to God and only
later counting the cost.

26 A wise king scatters the wicked
like wheat, then runs his
threshing wheel over them.

27 The LORD's light penetrates
the human spirit, exposing every
hidden motive.

28 Unfailing love and faithfulness
protect the king; his throne is
made secure through love.

29 The glory of the young is
their strength; the gray hair of
experience is the splendor of the
old.

30 Physical punishment cleanses
away evil; such discipline purifies
the heart.

Rash promise is foolish decision made without not enough consideration to what your thinking.

He sees all and knows all.

Young people are strong and full of energy. The old has their age to prove they have their experience.

Whoop-ins are not fun, but their necessary.

~NOTE SECTION~

It is What it is!!!

Proverbs 21

1 The king's heart is like a stream of water directed by the LORD; he guides it wherever he pleases.

2 People may be right in their own eyes, but the LORD examines their heart.

3 The LORD is more pleased when we do what is right and just than when we offer him sacrifices.

4 Haughty eyes, a proud heart, and evil actions are all sin.

God leads those in authority, no matter what position they may hold.

5 Good planning and hard work lead to prosperity, but hasty shortcuts lead to poverty.

6 Wealth created by a lying tongue is a vanishing mist and a deadly trap.

7 The violence of the wicked sweeps them away, because they refuse to do what is just.

8 The guilty walk a crooked path; the innocent travel a straight road.

9 It's better to live alone in the corner of an attic than with a quarrelsome wife in a lovely home.

10 Evil people desire evil; their neighbors get no mercy from them.

11 If you punish a mocker, the simpleminded become wise; if you instruct the wise, they will be all the wiser.

12 The Righteous One knows what is going on in the homes of the wicked; he will bring disaster on them.

13 Those who shut their ears to the cries of the poor will be ignored in their own time of need.

14 A secret gift calms anger; a bribe under the table pacifies fury.

Dads talk to your sons about this. If the Bible mentions, we know it's true.

15 Justice is a joy to the godly, but it terrifies evildoers.

It makes them see what they're doing is wrong.

16 The person who strays from common sense will end up in the company of the dead.

17 Those who love pleasure become poor; those who love wine and luxury will never be rich.

Because they waste their money on things they love.

18 The wicked are punished in place of the godly, and traitors in place of the honest.

19 It's better to live alone in the desert than with a quarrelsome, complaining wife.

I say again, pick your wife wisely.

20 The wise have wealth and luxury, but fools spend whatever they get.

Be responsible with your money.

21 Whoever pursues righteousness and unfailing love will find life, righteousness, and honor.

22 The wise conquer the city of the strong and level the fortress in which they trust.

23 Watch your tongue and keep your mouth shut, and you will stay out of trouble.

Mind your own business.

24 Mockers are proud and haughty; they act with boundless arrogance.

25 Despite their desires, the lazy will come to ruin, for their hands refuse to work.

Be a person of action.

26 Some people are always greedy for more, but the godly love to give!

27 The sacrifice of an evil person is detestable, especially when it is offered with wrong motives.

28 A false witness will be cut off, but a credible witness will be allowed to speak.

29 The wicked bluff their way through, but the virtuous think before they act.

30 No human wisdom or understanding or plan can stand against the LORD.

31 The horse is prepared for the day of battle, but the victory belongs to the LORD.

~NOTE SECTION~

Ways to Keep the Peace

Proverbs 22

1 Choose a good reputation over great riches;being held in high esteem is better than silver or gold.

2 The rich and poor have this in common: The LORD made them both.

3 A prudent person foresees danger and takes precautions. The simpleton goes blindly on and suffers the consequences.

Even tho your young, having a good name is good for you, it lets teaches and parents know they can trust you.

He doesn't favor one more than the others.

See the storm before it comes and be prepared for it.

4 True humility and fear of the LORD lead to riches, honor, and long life.

5 Corrupt people walk a thorny, treacherous road; whoever values life will avoid it.

6 Direct your children onto the right path, and when they are older, they will not leave it.

7 Just as the rich rule the poor, so the borrower is servant to the lender.

8 Those who plant injustice will harvest disaster, and their reign of terror will come to an end.

9 Blessed are those who are generous, because they feed the poor.

10 Throw out the mocker, and fighting goes, too. Quarrels and insults will disappear.

11 Whoever loves a pure heart and gracious speech will have the king as a friend.

12 The LORD preserves those with knowledge, but he ruins the plans of the treacherous.

13 The lazy person claims, "There's a lion out there! If I go outside, I might be killed!"

14 The mouth of an immoral woman is a dangerous trap; those

This is what we are doing with this book.

who make the LORD angry will fall into it.

15 A youngster's heart is filled with foolishness, but physical discipline will drive it far away.

16 A person who gets ahead by oppressing the poor or by showering gifts on the rich will end in poverty.

30 Sayings of the Wise

1. **17** 1Listen to the words of the wise; apply your heart to my instruction.

18 For it is good to keep these sayings in your heart and always ready on your lips.

19 I am teaching you today— yes, you— so you will trust in the LORD.

20 I have written thirty sayings for you, filled with advice and knowledge.

21 In this way, you may know the truth and take an accurate report to those who sent you.

2. **22** Don't rob the poor just because you can, or exploit the needy in court.

23 For the LORD is their defender. He will ruin anyone who ruins them.

3. **24** Don't befriend angry people or associate with hot-tempered people,

25 or you will learn to be like them and endanger your soul.

4. **26** Don't agree to guarantee another person's debt or put up security for someone else.

27 If you can't pay it, even your bed will be snatched from under you.

5. **28** Don't cheat your neighbor by moving the ancient boundary markers set up by previous generations.

6. **29** Do you see any truly competent workers? They will serve kings rather than working for ordinary people.

~NOTE SECTION~

Legacy

Fellowship, Food, and Money

7. Proverbs 23

1 While dining with a ruler, pay attention to what is put before you.
2 If you are a big eater, put a knife to your throat;
3 don't desire all the delicacies, for he might be trying to trick you.

8. 4 Don't wear yourself out trying to get rich. Be wise enough to know when to quit.

5 In the blink of an eye wealth disappears, for it will sprout wings and fly away like an eagle.

9. 6 Don't eat with people who are stingy; don't desire their delicacies.

7 They are always thinking about how much it costs. "Eat and drink," they say, but they don't mean it.

8 You will throw up what little you've eaten, and your compliments will be wasted.

10. 9 Don't waste your breath on fools, for they will despise the wisest advice.

11. 10 Don't cheat your neighbor by moving the ancient boundary markers; don't take the land of defenseless orphans.

11 For their Redeemer is strong; he himself will bring their charges against you.

12. 12 Commit yourself to instruction; listen carefully to words of knowledge.

13. **13** Don't fail to discipline your children. The rod of punishment won't kill them.

14. **14** Physical discipline may well save them from death.

15 My child, if your heart is wise, my own heart will rejoice!

16 Everything in me will celebrate when you speak what is right.

15. **17** Don't envy sinners, but always continue to fear the LORD.

18 You will be rewarded for this; your hope will not be disappointed.

16. **19** My child, listen and be wise: Keep your heart on the right course.

20 Do not carouse with drunkards or feast with gluttons,

21 for they are on their way to poverty, and too much sleep clothes them in rags.

17. **22** Listen to your father, who gave you life, and don't despise your mother when she is old.

23 Get the truth and never sell it; also get wisdom, discipline, an good judgment.

24 The father of godly children has cause for joy. What a pleasure to have children who are wise.

25 So give your father and mother joy! May she who gave you birth be happy.

26 O my son, give me your heart. May your eyes take delight in following my ways.

27 A prostitute is a dangerous trap; a promiscuous woman is as dangerous as falling into a narrow well.

28 She hides and waits like a robber, eager to make more men unfaithful.

29 Who has anguish? Who has sorrow? Who is always fighting? Who is always complaining? Who has unnecessary bruises? Who has bloodshot eyes?

30 It is the one who spends long hours in the taverns, trying out new drinks.

Description of people who drink too much and reason why you shouldn't.

31 Don't gaze at the wine,
seeing how red it is, how
it sparkles in the cup, how
smoothly it goes down.

32 For in the end it bites like
a poisonous snake; it stings
like a viper.

33 You will see hallucinations,
and you will say crazy
things.

34 You will stagger like a sailor
tossed at sea, clinging to
a swaying mast.

35 And you will say, "They
hit me, but I didn't feel it.
I didn't even know it when
they beat me up. When will
I wake up so I can look for
another drink?"

Things Alcoholics say:

~NOTE SECTION~

24

Reason to be Wise

Proverbs 24

20. **1** Don't envy evil people or
   desire their company.
   2 For their hearts plot
   violence, and their words
   always stir up trouble.
21. **3** A house is built by wisdom
   and becomes strong
   through good sense.
   4 Through knowledge its
   rooms are filled with all
   sorts of precious riches and
   valuables.

22. **5** The wise are mightier than the strong, and those with knowledge grow stronger and stronger.

6 So don't go to war without wise guidance; victory depends on having many advisers.

23. **7** Wisdom is too lofty for fools. Among leaders at the city gate, they have nothing to say.

24. **8** A person who plans evil will get a reputation as a troublemaker.

9 The schemes of a fool are sinful; everyone detests a mocker.

25. **10** If you fail under pressure, your strength is too small.

11 Rescue those who are unjustly sentenced to die; save them as they stagger to their death.

12 12 Don't excuse yourself by saying, "Look, we didn't know." For God understands all hearts, and he sees you. He who guards your soul knows you knew. He will repay all people as their actions deserve.

26. **13** My child, eat honey, for it is good, and the honeycomb is sweet to the taste.

14 14 In the same way, wisdom is sweet to your soul. If you find it, you will have a bright future, and your hopes will not be cut short.

27. **15** Don't wait in ambush at the home of the godly, and don't raid the house where the godly live.

16 The godly may trip seven times, but they will get up again. But one disaster is enough to overthrow the wicked.

28. **17** Don't rejoice when your enemies fall; don't be happy when they stumble.

18 For the LORD will be displeased with you and will turn his anger away from them.

29 **19** Don't fret because of evildoers; don't envy the wicked.

20 For evil people have no future; the light of the wicked will be snuffed out.

30. 21 My child, fear the LORD
and the king. Don't
associate with rebels,
22 for disaster will hit them
suddenly. Who knows what
punishment will come from
the LORD and the king?

More Sayings of the Wise

23 Here are some further sayings
of the wise: It is wrong to
show favoritism when passing
judgment.
24 A judge who says to the wicked,
"You are innocent," will be
cursed by many people and
denounced by the nations.
25 But it will go well for those who
convict the guilty; rich blessings
will be showered on them.
26 An honest answer is like a kiss of
friendship.
27 Do your planning and prepare
your fields before building your
house.
28 Don't testify against your
neighbors without cause; don't lie
about them.
29 And don't say, "Now I can pay
them back for what they've done
to me! I'll get even with them!"

30 I walked by the field of a lazy person, the vineyard of one with no common sense.

31 I saw that it was overgrown with nettles. It was covered with weeds, and its walls were broken down.

Effects of Being a Lazy Person.

32 Then, as I looked and thought about it, I learned this lesson:

33 A little extra sleep, a little more slumber, a little folding of the hands to rest—

34 then poverty will pounce on you like a bandit; scarcity will attack you like an armed robber.

~NOTE SECTION~

25

One Step at a Time

Proverbs 25

More Proverbs of Solomon

1 These are more proverbs of
   Solomon, collected by the
   advisers of King Hezekiah of
   Judah.
2 It is God's privilege to conceal
   things and the king's privilege to
   discover them.
3 No one can comprehend the
   height of heaven, the depth of the

earth, or all that goes on in the king's mind!

4 Remove the impurities from silver, and the sterling will be ready for the silversmith.

5 Remove the wicked from the king's court, and his reign will be made secure by justice.

6 Don't demand an audience with the king or push for a place among the great.

7 It's better to wait for an invitation to the head table than to be sent away in public disgrace. Just because you've seen something,

8 don't be in a hurry to go to court. For what will you do in the end if your neighbor deals you a shameful defeat?

9 When arguing with your neighbor, don't betray another person's secret.

10 Others may accuse you of gossip, and you will never regain your good reputation.

11 Timely advice is lovely, like golden apples in a silver basket.

12 To one who listens, valid criticism is like a gold earring or other gold jewelry.

13 Trustworthy messengers refresh like snow in summer. They revive the spirit of their employer.

Remove the bad things out of your life so you'll have room for the good.

Don't say, "Their doing it to" or "At least I'm not doing that, like them". If your both speeding don't get mad at them for not getting a caught.

14 A person who promises a gift but doesn't give it is like clouds and wind that bring no rain.

15 Patience can persuade a prince, and soft speech can break bones.

16 Do you like honey? Don't eat too much, or it will make you sick!

17 Don't visit your neighbors too often, or you will wear out your welcome.

18 Telling lies about others is as harmful as hitting them with an ax, wounding them with a sword, or shooting them with a sharp arrow.

19 Putting confidence in an unreliable person in times of trouble is like chewing with a broken tooth or walking on a lame foot.

20 Singing cheerful songs to a person with a heavy heart is like taking someone's coat in cold weather or pouring vinegar in a wound.

21 If your enemies are hungry, give them food to eat. If they are thirsty, give them water to drink.

22 You will heap burning coals of shame on their heads, and the LORD will reward you.

Did you hear that. Do your best to keep your word.

This scripture is an example of the saying, "Too much of anything thing isn't always good for you.

Don't wear out your welcome.

Don't tell lies.

Actions of forgiveness, and the results of them.

23 As surely as a north wind brings rain, so a gossiping tongue causes anger!

24 It's better to live alone in the corner of an attic than with a quarrelsome wife in a lovely home.

25 Good news from far away is like cold water to the thirsty.

26 If the godly give in to the wicked, it's like polluting a fountain or muddying a spring.

27 It's not good to eat too much honey, and it's not good to seek honors for yourself.

28 A person without self-control is like a city with broken-down walls.

Beware of Gossipers

Don't take on the worlds way of doing or believing in things.

There's no protection. Everything goes.

~NOTE SECTION~

Legacy

26

Comedic Wisdom for Everyday Living

Proverbs 26

1 Honor is no more associated with fools than snow with summer or rain with harvest.

2 Like a fluttering sparrow or a darting swallow, an undeserved curse will not land on its intended victim.

3 Guide a horse with a whip,
a donkey with a bridle, and a fool
with a rod to his back!

4 Don't answer the foolish
arguments of fools, or you will
become as foolish as they are.

5 Be sure to answer the foolish
arguments of fools, or they
will become wise in their own
estimation.

6 Trusting a fool to convey a
message is like cutting off one's
feet or drinking poison!

7 A proverb in the mouth of a fool
is as useless as a paralyzed leg.

8 Honoring a fool is as foolish as
tying a stone to a slingshot.

9 A proverb in the mouth of a
fool is like a thorny branch
brandished by a drunk.

10 An employer who hires a fool or
a bystander is like an archer who
shoots at random.

11 As a dog returns to its vomit, so a
fool repeats his foolishness.

12 There is more hope for fools than
for people who think they are
wise.

13 The lazy person claims, "There's
a lion on the road! Yes, I'm sure
there's a lion out there!"

It's there but it doesn't work for them.

Note-to-self

14 As a door swings back and forth on its hinges, so the lazy person turns over in bed.

15 Lazy people take food in their hand but don't even lift it to their mouth.

16 Lazy people consider themselves smarter than seven wise counselors.

17 Interfering in someone else's argument is as foolish as yanking a dog's ears.

Stay out of people business.

18 Just as damaging as a madman shooting a deadly weapon

19 is someone who lies to a friend and then says, "I was only joking."

20 Fire goes out without wood, and quarrels disappear when gossip stops.

21 A quarrelsome person starts fights as easily as hot embers light charcoal or fire lights wood.

22 Rumors are dainty morsels that sink deep into one's heart.

People who like to fight and has hatred in them.

23 Smooth words may hide a wicked heart, just as a pretty glaze covers a clay pot.

24 People may cover their hatred with pleasant words, but they're deceiving you.

25 They pretend to be kind, but
don't believe them. Their hearts
are full of many evils.

26 While their hatred may be
concealed by trickery, their
wrongdoing will be exposed in
public.

27 If you set a trap for others, you
will get caught in it yourself.
If you roll a boulder down on
others, it will crush you instead.

28 A lying tongue hates its victims,
and flattering words cause ruin.

~NOTE SECTION~

Bragging Rights

Proverbs 27

1 Don't brag about tomorrow, since you don't know what the day will bring.

2 Let someone else praise you, not your own mouth—a stranger, not your own lips.

3 A stone is heavy and sand is weighty, but the resentment caused by a fool is even heavier.

4 Anger is cruel, and wrath is like a flood, but jealousy is even more dangerous.

Resentment is a feeling you get after being done wrong. "Someone cheated you out of money or cheated on the game to beat you."

5 An open rebuke is better than hidden love!

6 Wounds from a sincere friend are better than many kisses from an enemy.

7 A person who is full refuses honey, but even bitter food tastes sweet to the hungry.

8 A person who strays from home is like a bird that strays from its nest.

9 The heartfelt counsel of a friend is as sweet as perfume and incense.

10 Never abandon a friend— either yours or your father's. When disaster strikes, you won't have to ask your brother for assistance. It's better to go to a neighbor than to a brother who lives far away.

Be this kind of friend.

11 Be wise, my child, and make my heart glad. Then I will be able to answer my critics.

From a dad's heart who is trying to raise his kids against the odds of the world.

12 A prudent person foresees danger and takes precautions. The simpleton goes blindly on and suffers the consequences.

13 Get security from someone who guarantees a stranger's debt. Get a deposit if he does it for foreigners.

Its saying to take something as collateral (Valuable) if you plan to co-sigh with someone.

14 A loud and cheerful greeting early in the morning will be taken as a curse!

15 A quarrelsome wife is as annoying as constant dripping on a rainy day.

16 Stopping her complaints is like trying to stop the wind or trying to hold something with greased hands.

17 As iron sharpens iron, so a friend sharpens a friend.

One of the purposes of this book, is to sharpen you into an individual.

18 As workers who tend a fig tree are allowed to eat the fruit, so workers who protect their employer's interests will be rewarded.

19 As a face is reflected in water, so the heart reflects the real person.

So True

20 Just as Death and Destruction are never satisfied, so human desire is never satisfied.

21 Fire tests the purity of silver and gold, but a person is tested by being praised.

22 You cannot separate fools from their foolishness, even though you grind them like grain with mortar and pestle.

23 Know the state of your flocks, and put your heart into caring for your herds,

24 for riches don't last forever, and the crown might not be passed to the next generation.

25 After the hay is harvested and the new crop appears and the mountain grasses are gathered in,

26 your sheep will provide wool for clothing, and your goats will provide the price of a field.

27 And you will have enough goats' milk for yourself, your family, and your servant girls.

This happens in business, when parents expect to pass down the family business or work to their kids.

Even tho things change and what use to be productive is gone, there is another opportunity to be productive.

~NOTE SECTION~

Legacy

Right and Wrong

Proverbs 28

1 The wicked run away when no one is chasing them, but the godly are as bold as lions.

2 When there is moral rot with in a nation, its government topples easily. But wise and knowledgeable leaders bring stability.

3 A poor person who oppresses the poor is like a pounding rain that destroys the crops.

4 To reject the law is to praise the wicked; to obey the law is to fight them.

5 Evil people don't understand justice, but those who follow the LORD understand completely.

6 Better to be poor and honest than to be dishonest and rich.

7 Young people who obey the law are wise; those with wild friends bring shame to their parents.

8 Income from charging high interest rates will end up in the pocket of someone who is kind to the poor.

9 God detests the prayers of a person who ignores the law.

10 Those who lead good people along an evil path will fall into their own trap, but the honest will inherit good things.

11 Rich people may think they are wise, but a poor person with discernment can see right through them.

12 When the godly succeed, everyone is glad. When the wicked take charge, people go into hiding.

13 People who conceal their sins will not prosper, but if they confess and turn from them, they will receive mercy.

14 Blessed are those who fear to do wrong, but the stubborn are headed for serious trouble.

15 A wicked ruler is as dangerous to the poor as a roaring lion or an attacking bear.

16 A ruler with no understanding will oppress his people, but one who hates corruption will have a long life.

17 A murderer's tormented conscience will drive him into the grave. Don't protect him!

18 The blameless will be rescued from harm, but the crooked will be suddenly destroyed.

Don't just dream, Act and Commit to doing something great.

19 A hard worker has plenty of food, but a person who chases fantasies ends up in poverty.

20 The trustworthy person will get a rich reward, but a person who wants quick riches will get into trouble.

21 Showing partiality is never good, yet some will do wrong for a mere piece of bread.

22 Greedy people try to get rich quick but don't realize they're headed for poverty.

23 In the end, people appreciate honest criticism far more than flattery.

Tell the truth in Loving Way.

24 Anyone who steals from his father and mother and says, "What's wrong with that?" is no better than a murderer.

25 Greed causes fighting; trusting the LORD leads to prosperity. Those who trust their own insight are foolish, but anyone who walks in wisdom is safe.

26 Whoever gives to the poor will lack nothing, but those who close their eyes to poverty will be cursed.

27 When the wicked take charge, people go into hiding. When the wicked meet disaster, the godly flourish.

~NOTE SECTION~

29

Don't Let it be You

Proverbs 29

1 Whoever stubbornly refuses to accept criticism will suddenly be destroyed beyond recovery.

2 When the godly are in authority, the people rejoice. But when the wicked are in power, they groan.

3 The man who loves wisdom brings joy to his father, but if he hangs around with prostitutes, his wealth is wasted.

4 A just king gives stability to his nation, but one who demands bribes destroys it.

5 To flatter friends is to lay a trap for their feet.

6 Evil people are trapped by sin, but the righteous escape, shouting for joy.

7 The godly care about the rights of the poor; the wicked don't care at all.

8 Mockers can get a whole town agitated, but the wise will calm anger.

9 If a wise person takes a fool to court, there will be ranting and ridicule but no satisfaction.

10 The bloodthirsty hate blameless people, but the upright seek to help them.

11 Fools vent their anger, but the wise quietly hold it back.

12 If a ruler pays attention to liars, all his advisers will be wicked.

13 The poor and the oppressor have this in common— the LORD gives sight to the eyes of both.

14 If a king judges the poor fairly, his throne will last forever.

15 To discipline a child produces wisdom, but a mother is disgraced by an undisciplined child.

16 When the wicked are in authority, sin flourishes, but

Discipline is necessary.

the godly will live to see their
downfall.

17 Discipline your children, and
they will give you peace of mind
and will make your heart glad.

18 When people do not accept
divine guidance, they run wild.
But whoever obeys the law is
joyful.

19 Words alone will not discipline
a servant; the words may be
understood, but they are not
heeded.

20 There is more hope for a fool
than for someone who speaks
without thinking.

21 A servant pampered from
childhood will become a rebel.

22 An angry person starts fights; a
hot-tempered person commits all
kinds of sin.

23 Pride ends in humiliation, while
humility brings honor.

24 If you assist a thief, you only hurt
yourself. You are sworn to tell the
truth, but you dare not testify.

25 Fearing people is a dangerous
trap, but trusting the LORD
means safety.

26 Many seek the ruler's favor, but
justice comes from the LORD.

27 The righteous despise the unjust;
the wicked despise the godly.

~NOTE SECTION~

30

Wisdom From a Guy Named Agur

Proverbs 30

The Sayings of Agur

1 The sayings of Agur son of Jakeh contain this message. I am weary, O God; I am weary and worn out, O God.

2 I am too stupid to be human, and I lack common sense.

3 I have not mastered human wisdom, nor do I know the Holy One.

4 Who but God goes up to heaven
and comes back down? Who
holds the wind in his fists? Who
wraps up the oceans in his cloak?
Who has created the whole wide
world? What is his name—and
his son's name? Tell me if you
know!

5 Every word of God proves true.
He is a shield to all who come to
him for protection.

6 Do not add to his words, or he
may rebuke you and expose you
as a liar.

7 O God, I beg two favors from
you; let me have them before
I die.

8 First, help me never to tell a lie.
Second, give me neither poverty
nor riches! Give me just enough
to satisfy my needs.

9 For if I grow rich, I may deny you
and say, "Who is the LORD?"
And if I am too poor, I may steal
and thus insult God's holy name.

10 Never slander a worker to the
employer, or the person will
curse you, and you will pay for it.

11 Some people curse their father
and do not thank their mother

12 They are pure in their own eyes,
but they are filthy and unwashed.

13 They look proudly around, casting disdainful glances.

14 They have teeth like swords and fangs like knives. They devour the poor from the earth and the needy from among humanity.

15 The leech has two suckers that cry out, "More, more!" There are three things that are never satisfied—no, four that never say, "Enough!":

16 1. the grave,
2. the barren womb,
3. the thirsty desert,
4. the blazing fire.

17 The eye that mocks a father and despises a mother's instructions will be plucked out by ravens of the valley and eaten by vultures.

18 There are three things that amaze me—no, four things that I don't understand:

19 1. how an eagle glides through the sky,
2. how a snake slithers on a rock,
3. how a ship navigates the ocean,
4. how a man loves a woman.

20 An adulterous woman consumes a man, then wipes her mouth and says, "What's wrong with that?"

21 There are three things that make
the earth tremble—no, four it
cannot endure:

22 1. a slave who becomes a king,
2. an overbearing fool who
prospers,

23 3. a bitter woman who finally
gets a husband,
4. a servant girl who supplants
her mistress.

24 There are four things on earth
that are small but unusually wise:

25 1. Ants—they aren't strong, but
they store up food all summer.

26 2. Hyraxes—they aren't
powerful, but they make their
homes among the rocks.

27 3. Locusts—they have no king,
but they march in formation.

28 4. Lizards—they are easy to
catch, but they are found even
in kings' palaces.

29 There are three things that walk
with stately stride—no, four that
strut about:

30 1. the lion, king of animals, who
won't turn aside for anything,

31 2. the strutting rooster,
3. the male goat,
4. a king as he leads his army.

Supplants means to supersede and replace.

32 If you have been a fool by being proud or plotting evil, cover your mouth in shame.

33 As the beating of cream yields butter and striking the nose causes bleeding, so stirring up anger causes quarrels.

~NOTE SECTION~

Alcohol and the Proverbs 31 Woman

Proverbs 31

The Sayings of King Lemuel

1 The sayings of King Lemuel contain this message, which his mother taught him.

2 O my son, O son of my womb, O son of my vows,

3 do not waste your strength on women, on those who ruin kings.

4 It is not for kings, O Lemuel, to guzzle wine. Rulers should not crave alcohol.

5 For if they drink, they may forget the law and not give justice to the oppressed.

6 Alcohol is for the dying, and wine for those in bitter distress.

7 Let them drink to forget their poverty and remember their troubles no more.

8 Speak up for those who cannot speak for themselves; ensure justice for those being crushed.

9 Yes, speak up for the poor and helpless, and see that they get justice.

A Wife of Noble Character

10 Who can find a virtuous and capable wife? She is more precious than rubies.

11 Her husband can trust her, and she will greatly enrich his life.

12 She brings him good, not harm, all the days of her life.

13 She finds wool and flax and busily spins it.

14 She is like a merchant's ship, bringing her food from afar.

15 She gets up before dawn to prepare breakfast for her household and plan the day's work for her servant girls.

Note-to-self: Don't allow this to worry you about other people who drink, let this be a warning to you.

16 She goes to inspect a field and buys it; with her earnings she plants a vineyard.

17 She is energetic and strong, a hard worker.

18 She makes sure her dealings are profitable; her lamp burns late into the night.

19 Her hands are busy spinning thread, her fingers twisting fiber.

20 She extends a helping hand to the poor and opens her arms to the needy.

21 She has no fear of winter for her household, for everyone has warm clothes.

22 She makes her own bedspreads. She dresses in fine linen and purple gowns.

23 Her husband is well known at the city gates, where he sits with the other civic leaders.

24 She makes belted linen garments and sashes to sell to the merchants.

25 She is clothed with strength and dignity, and she laughs without fear of the future.

26 When she speaks, her words are wise, and she gives instructions with kindness.

The Characteristics of a Proverbs 31 Woman.
- She makes her own clothes.
- She does her own shopping.
- She's an investor.
- Makes sure she doesn't lose money on her investments or businesses.
- She stays busy making stuff.
- She gives back to the community.
- She has everything her children needs.
- She decorates her home.
- Her husband is a community leader.
- She designs clothes.

27 She carefully watches everything in her household and suffers nothing from laziness.

28 Her children stand and bless her.
Her husband praises her:

29 "There are many virtuous and capable women in the world, but you surpass them all!"

30 Charm is deceptive, and beauty does not last; but a woman who fears the LORD will be greatly praised.

31 Reward her for all she has done. Let her deeds publicly declare her praise.

~NOTE SECTION~

Prayers Every Man Needs to Know

Prayer of Guidance

Psalm 23

1 A Psalm of David. The Lord is
my shepherd; I shall not want.

2 He makes me to lie down in green
pastures; He leads me beside the
still waters.

3 He restores my soul; He leads me
in the paths of righteousness For
His name's sake.

4 Yea, though I walk through the
valley of the shadow of death, I
will fear no evil; For You are with
me; Your rod and Your staff, they
comfort me.

5 You prepare a table before me in
the presence of my enemies; You
anoint my head with oil; My cup
runs over.

6 Surely goodness and mercy shall
follow me All the days of my life;
And I will dwell in the house of
the Lord Forever.

Psalms 23:1-6 (NKJV)

Prayer of Protection

Psalm 91

1 He who dwells in the secret place of the Most High Shall abide under the shadow of the Almighty.

2 I will say of the Lord, "He is my refuge and my fortress; My God, in Him I will trust."

3 Surely He shall deliver you from the snare of the fowler And from the perilous pestilence.

4 He shall cover you with His feathers, And under His wings you shall take refuge; His truth shall be your shield and buckler.

5 You shall not be afraid of the terror by night, Nor of the arrow that flies by day,

6 Nor of the pestilence that walks in darkness, Nor of the destruction that lays waste at noonday.

7 A thousand may fall at your side, And ten thousand at your right hand; But it shall not come near you.

8 Only with your eyes shall you look, And see the reward of the wicked.

9 Because you have made the Lord, who is my refuge, Even the Most High, your dwelling place,

10 No evil shall befall you, Nor shall any plague come near your dwelling;

11 For He shall give His angels charge over you, To keep you in all your ways.

12 In their hands they shall bear you up, Lest you dash your foot against a stone.

13 You shall tread upon the lion and the cobra, The young lion and the serpent you shall trample underfoot.

14 "Because he has set his love upon Me, therefore I will deliver him; I will set him on high, because he has known My name.

15 He shall call upon Me, and I will answer him; I will be with him in trouble; I will deliver him and honor him.

16 With long life I will satisfy him, And show him My salvation."

Psalms 91:1-16 (NKJV)

Prayer of Repentance

Psalm 51

1 To the Chief Musician. A Psalm of David when Nathan the prophet went to him, after he had gone in to Bathsheba. Have mercy upon me, O God, According to Your lovingkindness; According to the multitude of Your tender mercies, Blot out my transgressions.

2 Wash me thoroughly from my iniquity, And cleanse me from my sin.

3 For I acknowledge my transgressions, And my sin is always before me.

4 Against You, You only, have I sinned, And done this evil in Your sight--That You may be found just when You speak, And blameless when You judge.

5 Behold, I was brought forth in iniquity, And in sin my mother conceived me.

6 Behold, You desire truth in the inward parts, And in the hidden part You will make me to know wisdom.

7 Purge me with hyssop, and I shall be clean; Wash me, and I shall be whiter than snow.

8 Make me hear joy and gladness,
That the bones You have broken
may rejoice.

9 Hide Your face from my sins, And
blot out all my iniquities.

10 Create in me a clean heart, O
God, And renew a steadfast spirit
within me.

11 Do not cast me away from Your
presence, And do not take Your
Holy Spirit from me.

12 Restore to me the joy of Your
salvation, And uphold me by
Your generous Spirit.

13 Then I will teach transgressors
Your ways, And sinners shall be
converted to You.

14 Deliver me from the guilt
of bloodshed, O God, The
God of my salvation, And my
tongue shall sing aloud of Your
righteousness.

15 O Lord, open my lips, And my
mouth shall show forth Your
praise.

16 For You do not desire sacrifice,
or else I would give it; You do not
delight in burnt offering.

17 The sacrifices of God are a
broken spirit, A broken and a
contrite heart-- These, O God,
You will not despise.

18 Do good in Your good pleasure to Zion; Build the walls of Jerusalem.

19 Then You shall be pleased with the sacrifices of righteousness, With burnt offering and whole burnt offering; Then they shall offer bulls on Your altar.

Psalms 51:1-19 (NKJV)

The Lords Prayer

9 In this manner, therefore, pray:
Our Father in heaven, Hallowed
be Your name.

10 Your kingdom come. Your will be
done On earth as it is in heaven.

11 Give us this day our daily bread.

12 And forgive us our debts, As we
forgive our debtors.

13 And do not lead us into
temptation, But deliver us from
the evil one. For Yours is the
kingdom and the power and the
glory forever. Amen.

Matt 6:9-13 (NKJV)

~NOTE SECTION~

Message from the Author

I want you to know that I'm proud of you. I want you to know that you're needed. Man-to-Man, I want you to know that you're needed. Your intellect, your personality, and your strength are all needed in this world because you're special. There is a lot of hatred going around today that has been aimed and geared towards young men. Men who haven't done anything wrong or attempted to do anything wrong to anyone. I want you to know that it is going to take wisdom, knowledge, understanding, along with God's grace, favor, love, and protection for us to all live our lives. You "will" learn, hear about, and maybe even believe in different religions or methodologies, but I want you to always trust in God. Man-to-Man, I want you to believe in Jesus Christ.

I want you to learn to pray, learn to be okay with speaking to an invisible God who cares about you. You can start small by simply saying, "I need You, Lord," "Thank You, God," or "Lord, I need Your help." Move from there to the Lord's prayer a few pages to the left. By doing those simple actions, you will be on the road to developing a relationship with God. Legacy has almost one thousand Bible verses that can help you in life. Be wise, my son, trust God and continue on.

With much love and faith,
Benjamin D. Author

Conclusion

As we come to the end of this book, remember that **Wisdom** has no end. There will always be something we can learn. As you go from being a boy to a young man, a young man to a grown man, a grown man to an old man, the Word of the Lord is this: *Study this book of instructions continually. Meditate on it day and night so you will sure to obey everything written in it. Only then will you prosper and succeed in all you do. This is my command: be* **Strong and Courageous!** *Do not be afraid or discouraged. For the Lord your God is with you wherever you go.*

(Joshua 1:8-9 NLT)

www.ingramcontent.com/pod-product-compliance
Lightning Source LLC
Chambersburg PA
CBHW052043090426
42739CB00010B/2023